IMAGIN₍

In my time machin
I am free
No longer strapped
But able to drift, dri
Through the corridors of time
Across the barriers of space
To see things never seen before
Moving towards happiness
Coming to a brand new universe
Where I am free.

ALL THAT I AM

All that I am
My hopes and fears
Achievements and failures
Laughter and tears
Can be summed up
In the words I sing
Jesus
My Lord and King.

HOLY FIRE

Holy fire my desire
Come I yield my life to you
Holy fire my desire
Is to do the things I see you do
For you died to set me free
By your spirit make me what I should be
Holy fire my desire
Fill me with your love so true.

AT ANY MOMENT

At any moment
Love may come into your life
It may be a smile
A word
A common interest
Sharing a drink
When it happens
Receive it with joy
Take pleasure in its presence
For it is not ours to keep
You may wish the day not to end
But it must
And who knows about tomorrow
But there is this hope
Love once visited
May come again
This time to stay.

TRAFFIC LIGHTS

I wanted to make a start
To really go places
To meet lots of people
Friendly faces
I was full of ambition
A real go getter
Always looking for an angle
To make things better
But here in the traffic
I can't get ahead
The engine is revving
But the traffic lights are red.

DISTANT CRIES

You watch the TV
And hear the news
Comforted by experts
Soothed by their views.

It's not up to me
Is what you say
Leave it to God
It'll be ok.

But can't you see
You've been fooled by lies
And we can't wash our hands
Of the distant cries.

There's a need for action
That includes you and me
If we open our eyes
We will see.

He showed us the way
By his dying breath
And his power will give us
Victory over death.

EUROPE

I ordered egg and chips
And I got coq au vin
That's what happens when you join
The common market.

IF IT IS FRIDAY
IT MUST BE LIVERPOOL

If it is Friday
It must be Liverpool
It is so hard
To be your fool
But with your power
I know I can.

In this crowded carriage
Feeling all alone
I cannot understand
Why I am known
Just a mystery
That I am in your plan.

And I know when I get there
There is so much we can share
For broken hearts and lives
Will look to you.

So if it is Friday
It must be Liverpool
For you give me strength
And keep me cool
I will bring your love
To everyone.

SENSIBLE PEOPLE

Sensible people all around
Keeping their feet on the ground
Miracles a thing of the past
A change of heart will not last
But two thousand years it goes on
Despite discoveries love has not gone
Sensible people can't you see
He is the beginning of reality.

RETURN TICKET

I bought a ticket to paradise
But it caused me such pain
The ticket was a return
So I could not remain
Just as I was settling down
Looking forward to my food
Someone said the taxi is here
The awakening was quite rude
But I have another ticket
And this time I can stay
The Station Master paid for me
And it only goes one way.

LOVE LED ME ON

Love led me on
From my isolation
Broke through the walls
Of my frustration
Opened the door
And set me free
Caused me to blossom
And let me be me.

Love led me on
To people and places
Gave me acceptance
In welcoming faces
Made me feel valued
With a part to play
Filled me with hope
Each dawn and day.

VOICES

Waiting for an answer
The question not so clear
Voices are shouting
But I just can't hear
Give me your answer
Help me find the way
Too busy with word games
But some of us cannot play
Suddenly a new voice
Now I understand
No longer confusion
For you are in command.

RAP

Walking along
Singing a song
Feeling good
Like I know I should
Touched by your love
Heavens above
You set me free
So that I could see
How much you care
That you're always there
Blessing my life
You take away the strife
I have your peace
And I feel at ease
I know you died
But you're glorified
You conquered death
With your dying breath
And you rose again
And broke my chain
And you're always around
Like the sweetest sound
That's why I'm walking along
Singing this song.

A TOUCH OF LOVE

A touch of love is all I seek
To be accepted not seen as weak
A place of belonging where I am free
Won't someone reach out rescue me
A touch of love to save my life
When the pain of rejection cuts like a knife.

LIGHT

Darkness covers the earth
Hearts broken by hate
Dreams crumbled to dust
Fear resigns to fate
Hope turns to nightmare
Words of empty release
Pain is ever present
Never seems to cease
But wait
A voice
Singing in the night
Good news
For everyone
Here is light.

BEAUTY

Beauty is in the eye
Of the beholder
A slim figure
Trim face
Nimble waistline
We appreciate these
When figures bulge
Features fade
And nimble waists expand
The heart given to God
Endures forever.

I LOVE YOU WHEN
I am the way the truth and the life
If you will turn to me I will save you.
I know you have been looking
That your heart is sad.

I love you
When your heart is full of joy
When you want to dance and sing
When you want to speak of all that you see.
When you want to draw close
and share the wonders of creation.

I love you
When you feel heavy and sad.
When your hope is gone
When all you want to do is hide
To close your eyes
and to shut out the sounds of life.

I love you
When you show love for others
When you reach out in fellowship
When you share all the gifts that you have
Welcome brothers and sisters with open arms
With peace and love and hope.

I love you
When you can't face the person next to you
When you find it hard to talk to them.
When you would rather be alone
When tears choke your eyes
and when you can't take anymore.

My child look around
Do you not see
As I love you
So do they
Whether you are cross, or in love,
Whether you got out of the wrong side of bed,
or whether this is the first day of spring.
Whether you have just done an essay
or millions of books to read
They love you and you love them
We love each other
For love is what I give to you

YOUR LOVE

Your love touches deep within
Restoring my hope
I see the beauty
Transformed from darkness
Strength returns
And defeat recedes
Your love brings me to victory
And you.

EXILE

Where are the promises
I heard of in my youth
So many lies abound
I long to know the truth
Why has it all gone wrong
In this wilderness
I feel so alone
Father take me home

Restore again oh Lord
The days when we did sing
Let the sound of laughter
Through the city ring
Lord this exile is so long
Through this desert
I am forced to roam
Until you call me home.

Let your righteous anger
Turn to acts of love
Stretch out your hands to heal
Send peace as a dove
Then I will sing a different song
Show me your mercy
I bow before your thrown
For you have brought me home.

ONE DAY SOON

There's a bluebird flying high
It's wings touch the sky
And I want to follow
There's a sound in the air
Which isn't really there
And it sings down in the hollow
And my heart is so free
But my body waits for me

And I will fly
Rise up on eagle's wings
No longer tied by strings
One day soon

It will not be too long
'Til I sing a different song
And the world will ring with laughter
And the sun will shine all day
There'll be blue instead of grey
And love will reign for ever after
For His love has broke the chain
And taken all the pain.

TEN YEARS AFTER

Life changes
But still they stare
Talk in loud voices
Giggle behind hands
Converse with my keeper
I am still expected
To do nothing
To be happy and grateful
A symbol
Encouraging others
Life changes
But ten years after
It is still the same.

VALIUM BLUES

Well good grief, what's wrong with me?
I'm not shaking like a leaf,
Or bending like a tree,
I don't feel ill,
But I'd better take a pill
To help me sit still.

I was down in Wales and He said to me,
Look at Me, I can set you free,
I said, "O.k You're the boss"
He said, "Throw away", I said "What did You say?"
He said, "You can do it!", I said "Will I get through it?"
He said, "Throw away your pills, and cast away your ills!"

So I though about it, He said, "Go on, try it!"
"You can't talk about Me if you can't trust Me",
I said, "You know that's true"
So I threw them away and to this very day
I feel really free
So if you've got ills throw away your pills &
get hooked on Jesus instead.

EXCEPT FOR ACCESS

I could have danced on a stage
Sung songs of hope
Been an encouragement to friends
Performed a service for mankind
Scored a winning goal
Been a responsible citizen
Carried the hopes of the nation
Healed the wounded
I could have done great things
Except for access.

SEA BREEZES

I do like to be beside the sea-side
Watching the waves crash to shore
I do like to feel your love around me
And know I am secure.

SMILE

I like it when you smile
I forget for a while
The troubles in my life
The pain and the strife
Your eyes light up the sky
And I wonder why
You are able to rejoice
When you have no choice
Please tell me your secret
I promise I won't forget
What love is in your heart
And how did it start
Yes I like it when you smile
For you do it all the while

A SONG TO ALL DICTATORS AND TERRORISTS

Violence bloodshed hatred distress
The right to conquer command oppress
To destroy creation of nature and love
Sent down to earth from heaven above
War is your anthem
Death is your song
Don't sing it too loudly
Your hour is not long.

THE LITTLE PIECE OF PAPER

If I had time and space
I'd speak of love and the human race
I would surely remark
On Cleo's love for Mark
Other great loves there have been
Some you may have seen
Others you will never forget
Like Romeo and Juliet

But oh this piece of paper
Quickly begins to taper
And I with haste must race
To use up all the space
And yet things will have their way
Sufficient it is to say
I love you.

BEGINNINGS

When the snow falls down in August
When the sun doesn't shine in June
Then you know the long forgotten promises
Will come to pass very soon.

So many things seem to change today
And I'm not sure where I'm going
Ways that seem right, end in disaster
I'm scared to face what each new day will bring

I've heard there's a way to face the future
There isn't any anguish doubt or fear
And there's no place left to hide now I must decide
Seasons change the time is drawing near.

And it seems to me that the world is upside down
And all the things that we rely on lie shattered on the ground
So many questions and we haven't got a clue
And I begin to see it's true.

NAZARETH AGAIN

I came to you with a heart full of peace
A message of hope that will make your pain cease
But you wouldn't listen you turned me away
And told me to come back some other day.

Your eyes were filled with laughter mocking and scorn
When I said the night was over and soon there'd be dawn
And you thought you'd be alright and that you could cope
And it hurts me to see you resting on false hope.

Perhaps one day I'll be able to return
And your ears will be open ready to learn
Believe that I love you but I have to go
For there are many waiting and the truth they want to know

And standing in darkness
You can't see my pain
I'm feeling just like Jesus
It's Nazareth again.

LONGING

I have a longing
To be free
To be accepted
Seen as me
No longer guilty
But at peace
To see the battles
Within me cease
I have a longing
To be approved
Safe from danger
And always loved

ONE DAY

One day
I won't have to apologize
Cope with staring eyes
Be an object of pity
Have difficulty in the city.

One day
They will understand
The situation is in hand
That I really have a brain
Not an escapee from the insane

One day
I will be treated as human
The way God sees me now.

ARE THEY REALLY
He is a student you know
Is he really
With little speech
And no control
How on earth can that be

She is an athlete you know
Is she really
In her wheelchair
How can she compete
Well fancy that I do not see

They are married you know
Are they really
How do they cope
It must be hard
Not like you and me

They are human you know
Are they really.

ARMAGEDDON CALLING

I heard the news today
Troops are on the way
Just another power play
With different names.

Another crisis here
We have lost count this year
While East and West
Play the same old game.

New weapons build security
Preserve the life of the free
It's good for you
For you have no choice.

And those who disagree aren't heard
Love is treated like a dirty word
Might is right
No time for a quiet voice

The precipice is close at hand
But mocked are those who understand
But in that tragic final hour
We'll see who holds the real power
The one who's held it from the beginning.

And the peace that we are looking for
Is rapidly disappearing
Listen you can hear it on the wind
Armageddon calling.

WHO AM I

I ask the questions
That no one wants to know
I look for directions
Wondering where to go
I hope for fulfilment
A reason for being
But all I get is nothing
Like eyes never seeing
Tell me who am I
Why am I here
Do I have any value
Is there anybody there.

TOUCHED BY LOVE

Touched by love
And what was ugly
Turns to beauty.

Touched by love
Tears subside
Replaced by streams of joy.

For I find meaning in you
The world becomes a different place
Where I am at peace.

Touched by love
No longer guilty
Your power gives me life.

MIRROR IMAGE

In my weakness
I came to your window
But you turned away
Not wanting to know
You perceived my pain
And felt my despair
Acknowledged my existence
But wished me not there
You wrapped me in love
And hid me away
And thought to yourself
They have nothing to say
But as you start listening
And seek what is true
You look at my image
And find that it's you.

TAKE AND RECEIVE

Take and receive what I have to give
Take of my life so that you might live.

My heart is breaking and you will run away
But I will be waiting when the sun brings in the day.

One of you will betray me and one will deny
And darkness will surround you and you will cry.

So take and receive
My life for the world

That you might be whole
Take and receive
My life is nearly through
I give it up
To show I love you.

NORMAL PEOPLE

Your eyes say it is okay
Your smile bids stay a while
You feel safe
There is no danger
You give acceptance
Not seeing a stranger
But you have misread the story
And overlooked the twist
The trouble with normal people
Is they don't exist.

COMING

When he comes again
He will bring he sound of laughter
And the earth will sing with joy
The songs of old.

When he comes again
We will see his shining glory
And the shackles will be broken
We will be free.

When he comes again
To the sound of Hallelujah
The night will be destroyed
And day will come.

He will put an end to pain and sorrow
He will bring new hope for tomorrow
He will reign for ever
The king of kings
And lord of lords
Amen
When he comes again.

TURNING POINT

All my hopes lay broken
Scattered on the ground
The hopeful dreams of yesterday
Were nowhere to be found.

The loneliness around me
Was too much to bear
In my anguish I cried out
Is there anyone who cares.

It's so hard to understand
Why these things should be
But there is a point to all the sorrow
When wwe begin to see.

From tragedy comes triumph
And joy comes out of pain
For my hopes rise in the morning light
With you I live again.

I've gone as far as I can go
I don't feel I'll survive
But I have reached the turning point
And now I see that you're alive.

SILENT RAGE

How could this happen
Who can we blame
No matter what we try to do
The result is the same
Whatever happened to love
Peace and goodwill
Isn't life supposed to be precious
Why do we kill
Would the story be different
If we turned the page
Is anyone listening
To our silent rage.

FREEDOM SONG

I heard a distant thunder
As the earth began to shake
A sound of revolution in the air
The sky began to darken
And the sea began to roar
For the time of revelation is here.

Repression's hand was bleeding
And fear had run away
And the gates of death lay broken on the ground
And the prison of oppression
It's walls began to crack
As the final trumpet blasted out it's sound.

At the breaking of the morning
We stand ready to move
For there are those still fastened in chains
But the enemies of love
Are fleeing hour by hour
As they see the face of him who ends all pain.

For he is risen
And the grave has lost it's power
And we are waiting in the wings
For his triumphant hour.

And I was once a prisoner
In selfish agony
Heading for the dark world of night
And then he broke my bondage
My eyes began to see
And now I live in freedom's golden light

And will you still be chained
The dungeon yawning wide
Captivity for all eternity
Or will you turn to Jesus
And join our victory march
Come and sing the song of the free

And we shall rise like the sun
And it will not be too long
For no one can stop us
Sing our freedom song.

SIXTH COMMANDMENT

The glorious gift of nature
Is a present from the Lord
So why do we always
Put creation to the sword

We plough the fields and scatter
The good seed on the land
Then kill off all the creatures
Who lend a helping hand.

We all sit down to dinner
And eat up all the flesh
And sometimes in our conscience
We think of Bangladesh.

All crime shall be punished
And murderers shall die
But Jesus didn't say
Take an eye for an eye.

The battle which is won
The war which is lost
So many they are gone
So many count the cost.

Wars disease and weapons
Are not the only ills
Hatred lust and jealousy
Each one also kills.

There has to be an end
A stop to all bloodshed
Or else the world and life
Will very soon be dead.

Thou shall not kill
That's what the good Lord said
Thou shall not kill
So why are so many things dead.

THE CLOWN

The crowds have all gone home
In the ring he stands alone
His tricks have brought much laughter
Sad feelings always come after.

He is the clown
Who wears a comic crown
But no one sees inside
Where he tried to hide.

RELEASED

My eyes are open
And now I see
My chains are broken
Now I am free.

You came to my cell
And opened the door
You gave me your pardon
A prisoner no more.

I have been rescued
As in a fairy story
Now I can live
Just for your glory.

Now I am ready
To go to all nations
Give me your words Lord
I will sing of salvation.

When you touched me
All sorrow ceased
From the deepest dungeon
I am released.

WHY ME

Overtime at work
Wish that I could shirk
It's always the same
Always get the blame
Why me?

No time to spare
But they know I care
They never lend a hand
I don't understand
Why me?

Nailed to a cross
Suffering such great loss
When I look into his face
I see he is taking my place
Why me?

CHRISTMAS IS COMING

Christmas is coming
Soon we'll all be fat
A penny for the poor
The rest for your new hat.

King's carols on the radio
War on the telly
Fears about peace talks
Mixed with cream and jelly.

Jesus in a cowshed
Shivering from the cold
Children facing danger
With no chance to grow old.

It's just what I wanted
Think how much we will save
The shop is open tomorrow
We can swop the gift that Jesus gave.

CRYSTAL TEARS OF ETERNITY

I'm on my own again
My heart is full of pain
And where have all my dreams gone
I could smile yesterday
But the sun has gone away
And I wonder for how long
But I know he loves me
I have no need to fear
I am crying now
He will dry my eyes
For he keeps every crystal tea.

DREAMER

Your love goes on for ever
No matter what I do
Each day it comes with freshness
Just like the morning dew.

You don't see my shortcomings
There is no condemnation
And when the world is pressing in
You are there in my frustration.

The obstacles just melt away
Confronted by your power
And dreams turn into realities
With every passing hour.

They call me a dreamer
They say it won't come true
But when the doubts surround me
I see the truth in you.

DON'T FEED THE ANIMALS

Early morning at the station
Waiting for a train
Sorry nò facilities
Guard's van again
Cage is shut people walk
Things I have to bear
Trying to avert their eyes
Still they stand and stare
Back and forth they pass
Looking left and right
Please don't feed the animals
Or one day we might bite.

IT SHOULD HAVE BEEN DIFFERENT

It should have been different really
I think it's all gone wrong
The solution should have been easy
But it's taking far too long
I had the right intention
Determined to see it through
But something must be missing
I haven't got a clue
Yes
It should have been different really
And its making me feel blue
For I want to finish the job
But I don't know what to do.

DREAMS

I wanted to be
An engine driver
Breaking the speed record
Keeping to the timetable
But now I sit and wait
For a train which is late
Again.

FIRE

Touch my mouth
That I may speak
To broken hearts
Estranged and weak
The guilty ones
Who have no hope
Those holding on
To a fraying rope
Lift their eyes
From the mire
To see your love
A blazing fire.

ST. PANCRAS BLUES

Waiting for a train
Heart full of pain
Oh not again!
People crowd around
Hear the mournful sound
Strikes on the underground
More delays
And the tannoy keeps speaking
And it's all bad news
While I sit and wait
With St. Pancras blues.

SITTING

Sitting on a door step
Watching the world go by
No one seems to notice me
But I wonder why
Could it be I scare them
Because I am not the same
Perhaps the word spastic
Carries terror in it's name
If they would only listen
I would proclaim your loving care
Your power in hopelessness
And presence always there
But until their minds are open
They will only see the lie
So I will sit on the door step
And watch the world go by.

TERRACES

They came in thousands
To enjoy the game
They left in despair
Lives never the same
Like the crack of a whip
Bitter pain stings
Yet though crushed and broken
Still the spirit sings
And hope is still alive
Amidst the loss and pain
Like a phoenix from the ashes
Their song will rise again.

LOST DREAMS

What happened to the girl
Who grew into a princess
What happened to the genius
Destined for success
Where did happiness run to
And the sense of peace
Life full of riches
Nights of rest and ease
Lost dreams keep surfacing
Flush them down the drain
But love can revive them
And we can dream again.

IN EVERYTHING GIVE THANKS

When the road is steep and rocky
When the journey seems so long
Then I know that you are beside me
For you fill my heart with song.

There are times when I am happy
And everything is fine
But even when the sky is grey
You are with me all the time.

I have no fears for tomorrow
With Jesus as my friend
And one day I will see him face to face
At my journey's end.

And if the sun is shining
Or the rain is pouring down
With Jesus there beside me
I can face whatever comes
For his love gives me the strength to say
In everything give thanks.

FIVE MINUTES TO MIDNIGHT

I woke up this morning
Another dreary day
Somebody told me
War is on the way
Who has the answer
Where can we turn
Or will we be caught up
In the final burn

Politicians tell us
The future's bright
We are at the end of the tunnel
Walking in the light
But millions are starving
On television to view
And all the optimism
Seems so untrue.

Crises come so quickly
What happened to peace
Every day new tragedies
When will it cease
But in the midst of the darkness
There is a soft still voice
His hands are scarred and bleeding
But only we have the choice.

Five minutes to midnight
Who knows where we are going
How much time do we have left
Must we reap what we are sowing.

GUITAR

Guitar I see you standing there
Strings taut
Melody waiting to burst forth
Songs of joy straining to be
heard
One day I will play you.

THE DREAM

Laughed at
Stared at
Avoided and feared
Unusual
Astounding
To be shunned as weird
A painful encounter
A churning inside
Hurried conversation
They run away and hide
Silently wondering
Who is to blame
Funny when Jesus
Can accept me as I am
One day
My dream will come true
They you will see
I am just like you.

TRADING PLACES

If you were me
And I were you
There would be so much
That we could do
Climb a mountain
Sing a song
Fight good battles
Walk all day long
But that's not how
It is meant to be
Rejoice because
In God we see
He made you - you
And made me - me.

A LETTER TO SANTA

What do you want for Christmas
When Santa comes to call
Write your dreams in a letter
Maybe you'll get them all
A stereo music centre
A walking crying doll
A super duper video
A real leather football
Chart topping records
A bicycle to ride
Beer and fags for dad
For mum a handbag of real hide.

What would you like for Christmas
Little child so thin and small
With a voice so soft and gentle
Who is never heard at all
A crust of bread and water
An end to pain and fear
A promise from all governments
That we'll still be alive next year.

MISSED AGAIN

Your eyes sparkled across the room
I was captivated by your smile
We moved closer
But wheels
And footrests made it awkward
Cupid fired his arrows
But he missed again.

FIRST CLASS

Looking through the window
At the pleasant countryside
Rushing through the heather
Seeing Scotland's pride.

A week-end in Aberdeen
Going to see some friends
People all around me
Coping with sharp bends.

Sounds of joy and laughter
Appreciation of good food
Tourists over from the States
Don't want to be rude.

The hospitality is great
But I feel like little Jack Horner
Nobody seems to have time
For the table in the corner.

IN YOUR EYES

Oh what a hopeless case
An associate member of the human race
Little value anticipated
Kindly patiently tolerated
What future can there be
Achievement surely not a reality
No hope they do not fit
It is a shame and that is it
But you are the one who heals the pain
It's you who brings to life again
You break the barriers on every side
And welcome those who are denied
For you came to end the lies
And we are perfect in your eyes.

I THOUGHT THERE WAS A SANTA CLAUS

I thought there was a Santa Claus
Who rode upon a sleigh
And fulfilled all our wishes
On a snowy Christmas Day

They talked of red nosed reindeer
Of a secret place for toys
Of letters travelling through the air
From little girls and boys.

But when I opened up my sack
I did not get what I longed for
While everyone else was having fun
For me it was a bore.

It's nice to think we get
Our wishes fulfilled
But what about the war
And thousands being killed.

Yes I thought there was a Santa Claus
Who rode a magic sleigh
But I never got out of my wheelchair
On a snowy Christmas Day.

HALF LIGHT

The sun casts it's shadows
On scurrying people
For it is nearly time for tea
Reds and yellows
Highlight traffic jams
Shops begin to tidy up
And night stretches and yawns
For it is half light
And soon it will be dark

ENCOUNTER

Wandering lonely as a cloud
Looking for a point
Drifting endlessly in space
Like an addict with a joint
Suddenly I see a man
Nailprints in his feet and hands
Then I know he's calling me
I hear his commands
He touches deep inside
My heart is free again
His life he spent for me
To end all my pain.

WHEN CHILDREN CRY

When children cry
The sun hides
Rain pours down
Harmony turns to cacophony
And laughter runs away
For this is not how it should be
There should be joy
The sound of singing
A deep trust
And love
So don't let children cry.

WITH YOU

I can face the terrors
Of the darkest night
With my back against the wall
I will win the fight
Surround me with your love
And there's nothing I won't do
For you won the victory
I am alive with you.

A LOVE BEYOND COMPARE

They look at me with pity
They say such a shame
All his life in a wheelchair
Isn't anyone to blame.

They wonder how existence
Can be so endured
Or seek for an escape route
Wishing I were cured.

They only see the negative
Oh how will he cope
But my life is full of changes
That speak volumes of hope.

There is a power greater
Than any of life's pains
And even nailed to a wooden tree
He broke oppression's chains.

Nothing is impossible
When love is on your side
He has opened every door
And I am free to ride.

Please open up your heart
There's so much I can share
I found meaning to my life
In a love beyond compare.

HANDS OF THE CLOCK

Waiting for something to happen
Sitting with bated breath
Watching the seconds tick by
As slowly as death
Frustration like a tap dancer
Makes a heavy sound
Hopes struggle to reach the sky
Like heavy weights pressed to the ground
But the hands of the clock are relentless
Though sometimes it's hard to see
And our trust is never in vain
For our longed for dreams we shall see.

HOW CAN THEY REFUSE

If they could see
Your love for me
Your presence every day
Which gives me hope
So I can cope
Whatever comes my way.

If they could feel
Your loss and pain
And touch your heart of grief
They wouldn't hide
From him who died
Or live in unbelief.

And when they know
The hurt you bear
Hatred and abuse
The prize you won
Through your own son
How can they refuse.

GO

They say I am a failure
A hopeless waste
An object of pity
Rejected
They wonder how I can cope
Feel sorry for me
Pat me on the head
Offer to buy me an ice cream
But they never talk to me
Did you have a good holiday
Do you really travel alone
You are brave
So clever
But there is one who commands me to go
And tell of his love
No matter what obstacles
I will go in his power from above.

SO WHAT NOW?

So what now?
Do I walk away
Save your love
For a rainy day
Programme time
In my filofax
Treat it all
As just old hat
But what about the fact
Of your generous a act
Dying in my place
To take away disgrace
Surely I can't forget
Your love is calling yet
So what now
I give my life to you.

KNOWING

Knowing me knowing you
I find your love is true
Even in the depths of despair
When I call I know you are there
Even before my life began
You had already formed your plan
There is nowhere I can go
Whether high or whether low
Knowing how much
You love me
There is nowhere else
I would rather be.

INNOCENT BLOOD

The cry of the innocent
Hangs in the air
Shrieks of terror
A rage of fear
Exploitation
Abuse
Mistrust
Beauty defiled
Love turned to lust
So save our children
From this carnage
Let's have no more
Of this ruthless damage
God keeps his record
Of bad and good
And he hears the wailing
Of innocent blood.

NOT YET

I would like to run along the shore
To dance skip and jump
Ride a horse, kick a ball
Use my hands for good
Not yet.

I would like to sing songs of joy
Play music on my guitar
Have a voice both loud and clear
Take the message far
Not yet.

I would like to be like Jesus
And never go astray
Have an answer to all the questions
I meet from day to day
Not yet.

Sometimes the frustration brings me near to tears
Then my mind is restless filled with doubt and fear
But there is a voice inside me who renews my hope
Turning doubt to certainty and with Him I can cope

There is no other way to live
Only by his grace
One day all the things I hope for
I will see before my face
And not yet will be over.

DREAMING

I'm dreaming of happiness
A life full of ease
Purpose and contentment
Laughter and peace
A comfortable existence
With treasure every day
But how can I find it
Who knows the way.

SHOPPING

Home again
A cup of tea
Now the rush is all over
Check the list
With satisfaction
Feeling all in clover
Cards and stuffing
Pipes for puffing
Fairy lights and tree
Turkey crackers scarlet ribbons
Drinks and guide to the TV
Yes it is all here
Nothing left to remember
But what are we going to do
For the rest of September.

REFUGE

When the world asks too much
And I cannot cope
When I'm feeling alone
And losing hope
When I wonder how long
Before the dream comes true
When frustrations surround me
I look to you
And your love
Like a river
Overflows
Fills me with confidence
Helps my faith grow
For I know you will keep me
In the midst of the deluge
Safe in your arms
For you are my refuge.

MIDNIGHT

Shadows hover
Shrieks of pain
Demons rattle
Heavy chains
An icy finger
Down the spine
Your reflection
Or is it mine
Midnight comes
To bring us fear
But it fails
For you are near.

END OF SUMMER

End of summer
And leaves begin to crinkle
The sun thinks about flying south
For a mid winter break
Holiday romances are forgotten
Despite promises to write
Hopes and dreams are put away
In cases for next year
And only photographic memories
Keep alive our hope
That summer will come again.

DIRTY HANDS

Dirty hands, dirty hearts
This is where the trouble starts
Filled with bitterness and spite
Not caring if it's wrong or right
Greedy desires to make things bigger
Itchy fingers on the trigger
Life is cheap it doesn't matter
Place the bomb and watch them scatter
But wise is he who understands
His blood has cleansed our dirty hands.

INSANITY

Twenty thousand soldiers
Marching as to war
Banners flying high
Mighty cannons roar.

Twelve thousand soldiers
Won't come home again
Pride has turned to shame
Joy has turned to pain.

Eight thousand soldiers
Marching home to stay
The game is called insanity
And anyone can play.

A BIG MAC SATURDAY

Munching a quarter pounder
Sitting in a corner
Waiting for coffee
That never seems to cool
Surrounded by High Street people
Confronted by choice
Upstairs, downstairs,
A desperate milkshake
Decides to commit suicide
By jumping into a shopping bag
Frantic parents
Encourage children to behave
With threats of death or worse
The lady with the mop
Provides a regular service
Washing the floor
And customers feet
Meanwhile Donna wipes the tables
And wonders if there could be
More to life than this.

DANCER

The music stirs
Rhythms haunting
But a simple task
Seems so daunting
He longs to fly
To break the air
But tied to the spot
In his wheelchair
The dancer sits
And waits for the day
When with his love
He will waltz away.

LAMENT

Working for the Lord
The pay may not be good
But there are compensations
Like friendship and lots of food.

Coffee morning over
Waiting eagerly for lunch
Anticipation high
Tasty morsels to munch

The fare is set before us
And joy is tinged with pain
I can't believe my eyes
Quiche and salad yet again!

SATURDAY LITTLE CHEF

Please can I have the frank
I don't want to call it bill
Because when I see the prices
I know that I'll be ill
After all that time in the queue
It was nice to get the weight off our feet
And it only took half an hour
Before we started to eat
They said it wouldn't be long
And so I held my breath
But I nearly died of heart failure
Saturday at Little Chef.

DON'T TALK TO ME ABOUT LIFE

Don't talk to me about life
I think it's just a joke
And I don't like the punch line
It makes me want to choke
Please stop talking
I don't want to hear
The truth might make me think
And that is what I fear
Don't talk to me about life
I really can't face it today
I'd have to make a decision
And live a different way.

AM I AN ACCIDENT

They tell me I'm an accident
That is why I'm here
A succession of chances
Which is very rare
A mixture of gasses
Molicules and parts
A hit and miss affair
With many stops and starts
But if I am an accident
Can someone tell me why
I have such concern
About if I live or die.

THE LIGHT AT THE END OF THE TUNNEL

The light at the end of the tunnel
Keeps shining bright
My eyes are fixed upon it
In the darkest night
Sometimes I think it's fading
And it may die
Then I start to worry
My heart begins to cry
But when I look again
I see it is still on
And I will walk towards it
Until my fears are gone.

SECURE

When the waves crash against the shore
When my hopes collapse
And I feel unsure
Your love surrounds me
Bringing new hope
Your strength within me
Then I can cope
For your promises stand
And your word endures
And your peace like a fortress
Means that I am secure.

LOVE TAKES MY HAND

Love takes my hand
And I can stand
My foot upon the rock
What ever the knock
You forgive my ways
And fill my days
With sweet success
Tears and happiness
Your love takes my hand
Then I understand
How much you love me.

A KNOCK AT THE DOOR

There's a knock at the door
And my hand is on the chain
I hear it rattle
Here it comes again
Have I got the courage
To open the door
Will there be any difference
Or just like it was before
What shall I do
Can he end my strife
Shall I open up
And receive his life.

BUT FOR YOU

But for you
I would have given up
Run away in retreat
Died of frustration
Accepted defeat
Turned to crime
Or selfish greed
Exploited others
Become a priority need
But I saw your scars
And your bloody wound
And you changed my heart
My life, my moods
But for you
That's how I would be
But because of you
I am free.

YOU ARE MY LIGHT

You touched my life
And chains fell apart
Fears ran away
You revived my heart
Took what was broken
And made it new
Gave me fulfilment
I trust in you
When I feel hopeless
And full of pain
You calm my fears
Reassure me again
That you will never leave me
In the midst of the fight
In my darkest hour
You are my light.

LOVE IN A DYING WORLD

Take a look around you
Tell me what you see
Fear on every face
How can that be
Clouds of dark pollution
Choking up the sky
Who has the solution
Many voices cry.

And it's no good to look away
You know there's a better way
We need love in a dying world
Today

There is so much starvation
What on earth can we do
Leave it to the authorities
Forget about me and you
But every time we show love
A miracle occurs
And our complacent indifference
Only makes it worse.

Let love be genuine
No more selfish pride
We need to look to others
And take their side
There's a man way back in time
Who showed us the way
Gave his life for love
We need to give our love away.

NO ONE WILL TAKE YOUR LOVE AWAY

Of all the love
I've ever had before
I give you everything
You gave me so much more
All the doubts have gone
Of you I am sure
That your love is the best.

You pick me up
From the cold hard ground
Dazed and confused
You brought me round
Turned away the nightmare
With love's sweet sound
And in you I rest.

Hold me close to you
Through the longest night
I fear no enemy
You have won the fight
From the darkness of loneliness
You gave me sight
Jesus I need your love.

Whatever the problems I meet from day to day
No one will take your love away.

TV DINNER

Let's buy a TV dinner
Then we can watch the war
Marvel at the technology
At sights never seen before
And as we eat our food
And watch it round the clock
The taste will give us comfort
And wash away the shock.

NO COMPROMISE

No compromise
We stare across the table
Blaming each other
Eyes like daggers
Not seeking forgiveness or reconciliation

No compromise
As miliary force gathers
With weapons of distruction
Pushing diplomacy
To the background.

No compromise
As nails are driven into hands
Tongues speak words of hate
And he dies
For all.

THE CLUB

I was going to be a human
But they wouldn't let me in
They said I was a fire risk
My brain was much too thin.

They could not get me up the steps
So they closed the door
Suggested that a country club
Would probably suit me more.

But as I rolled back down the hill
Floating in my tears
I noticed Jesus was coming too
He's been trying to get in for years.

REVELATION

You think I am your worst nightmare
A total catastrophe
When you look at me you feel ill
And wonder how such a thing
Could happen
If God is love
The cost is too high
And yet guilt forces you
To try contact
Then you discover
I am like you.

FOR YOU

All alone on a stage
I see them sit and stare
See their puzzled faces
An enigma in a wheelchair.

You took my broken body
And made me live again
You give me power to cope
In frustration fear and pain.

Sometimes I do not understand
The things you make me do
The odds are all against me
And yet you bring me through.

They only see the laughter
You wipe away the tears
It's you who picks me up
When I am drowning in my fears.

And though there may be problems
I know your love is true
And whatever I may face
I'll do anything for you.

ABOUT ALYN HASKEY

Born with Cerebral Palsy, Alyn spent his early years fighting against severe disability, including a serious speech defect. Education was considered a waste of time for him, and frequent changes of schools resulted in little progress.

Then at the age of fourteen Alyn became a Christian. His life began to change. He gained O and A level qualifications before going on to university to take a degree in History and Sociology. Since then he has studied for a Licentiate in Theology, as well as attaining a B.A. with the Open University.

Alyn's life is not all study, however. He has a keen interest in sport - not only watching but also competing. He has represented Great Britain in the disabled Olympics, and travelled overseas several times in the hunt for medals. Never content to relax, Alyn has also gained the bronze, silver and gold medals for the Duke of Edinburgh's Award.

Alyn's first love, however, is his work for the Lord. He describes himself as a poet and evangelist. He has written and published various books including an autobiography. Despite being confined to a wheelchair, Alyn travels widely, and likes nothing better than discussing and sharing what Jesus can do for anyone who puts their trust in Him.

This work has taken Alyn into schools, colleges, churches - wherever people get together. He is more than willing to preach, take services, help lead missions, or speak to small groups. In fact, Alyn is willing to have a go at anything he's asked to do, so long as it is within the bounds of possibility (and sometimes when it isn't!)

MOORLEY'S

are growing Publishers, adding several new titles to our list each year. We also undertake private publications and commissioned works.

Our range of publications
Includes: **Books of Verse**
    Devotional Poetry
    Recitations
    Drama
    Bible Plays
    Sketches
    Nativity Plays
    Passiontide Plays
    Easter Plays
    Demonstrations
    Resource Books
    Assembly Material
    Songs & Musicals
    Children's Addresses
    Prayers & Graces
    Daily Readings
    Books for Speakers
    Activity Books
    Quizzes
    Puzzles
    Painting Books
    Daily Readings
    Church Stationery
    Notice Books.
    Cradle Rolls
    Hymn Board Numbers

Please send a S.A.E. (approx 9" x 6") for the current catalogue or consult your local Christian Bookshop who should stock or be able to order our titles.